"IT'S NOT COMMON SENSE, IT'S SOFT SKILLS"

ACTIVITY

BOOK

PMD Professional Mindset Development

It's Not Common Sense, It's Soft Skills!!
By: Professional Mindset Development

Published by:
VJ PUBLISHING HOUSE, LLC.
67 N.W. 183 rd STREET SUITE V9
MIAMI GARDENS, FL. 33169
PHONE: 786-303-9551

www.vjpublishinghouse.com
vjpublishinghouse@gmail.com

Paperback ISBN#: 978-1-939236-27-2
(Student Activity Workbook)

Acknowledgments

A special thanks to Amanda Matos for her exceptional work in designing the cover of this manual.

The information compiled in these pages was enriched by the valuable input of both teachers and students, whose perspectives helped shape the content into a practical and engaging resource.

Special thanks to Sasha Fernandez, a graduate of Barron Collier High School, and Christian Paul, a current student at Barron Collier High School in Naples, FL, for their creativity, dedication, and valuable contributions in designing the layouts and providing thoughtful, innovative input throughout the process.

Table of Contents

It's Not Common Sense,
It's Soft Skills

Preface

Wait... what even are Soft Skills?

Let me tell you a little story.

During one winter break, my 21-year-old son came home from college, where he was pursuing not one but three majors: marketing, computer science, and economics. His brain is like a creativity blender, always on overdrive, and I've always thought he was natural in marketing. So, I handed him a copy of my soft skills curriculum, showed him my new website, super excited to get his genius feedback.

He flipped through it... looked confused... and then said:

"I don't get it. Why are you making such a big deal about this?" Cue dramatic gasp! I was so crushed.

But the next day, he texted me a video he saw on TikTok. It was a girl talking about her internship experience at a financial company, saying how she wished someone had taught her soft skills in school because they would've helped her way more than she realized.

Suddenly, a light bulb went off.

Flash forward to that summer—my son's interning at Visa, surrounded by other brilliant minds. Everyone had tech know-how. But he told me: "What set me apart wasn't what I knew. It was how I connected with people."

And that, my friends, is why this workbook exists. Because someday, you will be in a room full of people with the same knowledge, same qualifications, maybe even the same GPA.

But what will make you shine like the rock star you are?

It is your *soft skills*—like empathy, communication, problem-solving, and leadership.

Let's get started.

Module 1
Communication Activity Guide

Scoop of the day

What is communication?

Communication is the ability to share information, ideas, and emotions effectively. It's more than just talking!

☑ Verbal communication: It is what you say!

☑ Non-verbal communication: It is facial, vocal, and body cues!

☑ Written communication: It is what you write!

Why does it matter?

How does communication help in life or work?

Strong communication makes teamwork easier, helps you lead, and solves problems. Whether you're in a restaurant, hospital, law office, or tech company—communication is key!

Think...

Write your ideas about why communication matters in the job:

_____

_____

Mind expeditions

Draw: Create a map showing how communication connects to teamwork, leadership, and success.

(Use circles, lines, and arrows!)

What would you do?

Scenario: You're working in a busy restaurant kitchen during the dinner rush. The chef shouts: "Two medium-rare steaks, one with mashed potatoes, one with roasted vegetables, and a side of garlic bread—fire now!" You miss part of it because of the noise.

Do you guess?

Do you ask for clarification?

How will you communicate under pressure?

💬 Write your ideas....

_____

_____

Real-world examples...

Law: Lawyers explain tricky terms in ways clients can understand.

Healthcare: Pharmacists give clear instructions about medicine.

Sales: Reps pitch products so customers want to buy.

Write an example!

Write your own example of communication at work:

_____

_____

AI Prompt Exercise...

Write an AI prompt that is clear, specific, and detailed enough to help you get the best possible answer.

Scenario: Your class is planning a fundraiser, but people are not signing up to help. Write a short announcement or social media post to inspire more volunteers.

_____

_____

Module 2
Professionalism Activity Guide

Scoop of the day

What is professionalism?

Professionalism means acting responsibly, ethically, and respectfully at work.

- ☑ Reliability & accountability
- ☑ Positive attitude & respect
- ☑ Handling issues with maturity
- ☑ Proper appearance
- ☑ Good time management

Why does it matter?

How does professionalism help in life or work?

- Build trust with coworkers.
- Show you're dependable.
- Standout especially when using AI and technology tools.

Think...

How can professionalism give you an edge in your career?

_____

_____

Mind expeditions

Mind Map: Below, draw or list how professionalism connects to skills like communication and teamwork.

What would you do?

Scenario: You're in a meeting. Your manager shares a plan with a major flaw. No one else mentions it. Do you guess?

- Speak up now or later?

- How do you share your concern without sounding rude?

- How can you be taken seriously?

Write your ideas....

_____

_____

Real-world examples...

Finance: Analysts present data professionally.

Education: Teachers plan lessons and communicate with parents.

Creative: Designers meet deadlines and handle feedback.

Write an example!

Write your own example of professionalism at work:

_____

_____

AI Prompt Exercise...

Write an AI prompt that is clear, specific, and detailed enough to help you get the best possible answer.

Scenario: Ask AI for five tips on making a positive first impression during a school interview or meeting with a guest speaker.

_____

_____

Module 3
Work Ethic Activity Guide

Scoop of the day

What is work ethic?

Work ethics means showing dedication, responsibility, and commitment to your job.

- ☑ Being reliable & on time
- ☑ Taking initiative
- ☑ Acting with honesty & integrity
- ☑ Meeting deadlines
- ☑ Working hard without constant supervision

Why does it matter?

How does professionalism help in life or work?

- Build stronger relationships.
- Avoid misunderstandings.
- Standout—especially in workplaces using AI and fast-changing technology.

Think...

How does having a strong work ethic give you an advantage? What are some habits that reflect a strong work ethic?

_____

_____

Mind expeditions

Ethics in Action: Analyze a workplace scenario. What's the right thing to do? What are the consequences of ignoring problems?

What would you do?

Scenario: You see a coworker clock in but not start working on time. It keeps happening.

- Do you talk to the coworker or report it?

- How do you handle it respectfully?

- What happens if you ignore it?

💬 Write your ideas....

_____

_____

Real-world examples...

Finance: Advisors stay transparent with clients.

Healthcare: Doctors follow strict ethical standards.

Retail: Employees report theft to protect the company.

Write an example!

Describe a time when someone showed strong work ethic.

_____

_____

AI Prompt Exercise...

Write an AI prompt that is clear, specific, and detailed enough to help you get the best possible answer.

Scenario: Ask AI to create a daily schedule to balance school, homework, a part-time job, and extracurricular activities.

_____

_____

Module 4
Problem-Solving Activity Guide

Scoop of the day

What is problem-solving?

Problem-solving means identifying, analyzing, and resolving challenges effectively.

☑ Critical thinking   ☑ Decision-making

☑ Creativity   ☑ Adaptability

Why does it matter?

How does problem-solving help in life or work?

- Keep projects moving.
- Handle unexpected issues.
- Standout—especially in workplaces that use AI and technology.

Think...

How can problem-solving skills give you an advantage in your career?

_____

_____

Mind expeditions

Role-play Activity: Act out a situation where a group faces a challenge (like missing supplies or a tight deadline). First, show the group reacting poorly. Then "rewind" and work together to solve the challenge. Reflect on what changed and how it was effective below:

What would you do?

Scenario: You're on a team project. Two teammates strongly disagree on how to proceed. The conflict is delaying progress, and deadlines are approaching.

- How do you mediate without taking sides?

- What steps help keep the project on track?

- How can you encourage teamwork and find a solution?

💬 Write your ideas....

_____

_____

Real-world examples...

Engineering: Solving a technical issue delaying a bridge project.

Customer Service: Fixing delivery delays in the supply chain.

Event Planning: Reorganizing an event after a speaker cancels.

Write an example!

Describe a problem and how you would solve it:

_____

_____

AI Prompt Exercise...

Write an AI prompt that is clear, specific, and detailed enough to help you get the best possible answer.

Scenario: Your school's vending machines keep breaking. Brainstorm three possible solutions and explain which is best and why.

_____

_____

Module 5
Critical Thinking Activity Guide

Scoop of the day

What is critical thinking?

Critical thinking means analyzing information, questioning assumptions, and making sound decisions.

- ☑ Logic and reasoning
- ☑ Evaluating different viewpoints
- ☑ Making fact-based conclusions

Why does it matter?

How does critical thinking help in life or work?

- Making smart decisions.
- Avoid mistakes based on bias or incomplete information.
- Standout—especially when using AI and data tools.

🧠 Think...

How does critical thinking give you an advantage at work?

_____

_____

Mind expeditions

Draw: Using a Venn Diagram, compare Critical Thinking and Problem-Solving (What's the same? What's different?)

What would you do?

Scenario: Your company may buy new software to boost efficiency. The sales rep shares lots of positives, but you notice missing details like long-term costs and compatibility.

- What questions would you ask?

- How would you weigh pros and cons?

- How do you avoid being swayed by sales tactics?

💬 Write your ideas....

_____

_____

Real-world examples...

Healthcare: Doctors analyze symptoms to diagnose conditions.

Marketing: Teams study data to improve campaigns.

Education: Teachers adjust lessons based on student progress.

Write an example!

Describe a time when critical thinking helped solve a problem.

_____

_____

AI Prompt Exercise...

Write an AI prompt that is clear, specific, and detailed enough to help you get the best possible answer.

Scenario: Your school wants to switch to only digital textbooks. Analyze potential benefits and drawbacks.

_____

_____

Module 6
Teamwork Activity Guide

Scoop of the day

What is teamwork?

Teamwork and collaboration mean working well with others to reach a shared goal.

- ☑ Clear communication

- ☑ Flexibility & adaptability

- ☑ Cooperation & support

Why does it matter?

How does teamwork help in life or work?

- Solving problems faster.
- Build trust and respect.
- Succeed in any career, especially with AI and new technology tools.

Think...

How can teamwork skills give you an edge at work?

_____

_____

Mind expeditions

Role-play Activity: In a group, act out a short scene where one person takes over and ignores everyone. Arguments ensue. Then "rewind" and use the skills we've learned to show how to collaborate effectively. Reflect on what changed below:

What would you do?

Scenario: Your team has a big project with a tight deadline. One teammate is falling behind, and the rest of the group is frustrated. What questions would you ask?

- How do you help your teammate without doing their work?

- What can you do to keep the team motivated?

- How do you talk about the issue respectfully?

💬 Write your ideas....

_____

_____

Real-world examples...

Technology: Software teams build apps together.

Healthcare: Surgeons and nurses coordinate during surgeries.

Film: Directors and actors collaborate to make movies.

Write an example!

Describe a time when teamwork made a difference.

_____

_____

AI Prompt Exercise...

Write an AI prompt that is clear, specific, and detailed enough to help you get the best possible answer.

Scenario: A team member dominates every discussion. Draft a respectful way to encourage equal participation.

_____

_____

Module 7
Active Listening Activity Guide

Scoop of the day

What is active listening?

Active listening means focusing fully, understanding, and responding thoughtfully in conversations.

- ☑ Paying attention.
- ☑ Showing empathy.
- ☑ Asking questions to clarify.

Why does it matter?

How does active listening help in life or work?

- Build stronger relationships.
- Avoid misunderstandings.
- Standout—especially in workplaces using AI and fast-changing technology.

Think…

How can active listening skills give you an edge at work?

_____

_____

Mind expeditions

Role-play Activity: In a group, act out a short scene where one person isn't actively engaging with the other, creating a baffling misunderstanding. Then "rewind" and show how active listening avoided a confusing situation. Reflect on what changed and how it was more effective:

What would you do?

Scenario: During a meeting, your manager explains a new workflow. A coworker asks a question that was already answered, slowing the discussion. How do you help your teammate without doing their work?

- How can you make sure you're listening carefully?

- How could you help your coworker without embarrassing them?

- What strategies help you stay focused?

💬 Write your ideas....

_____

_____

Real-world examples...

HR: Listening to employees during mediation.

Healthcare: Therapists listening to patients.

Retail: Managers hearing team feedback.

Write an example!

Describe a time when active listening helped solve a problem.

_____

_____

AI Prompt Exercise...

Write an AI prompt that is clear, specific, and detailed enough to help you get the best possible answer.

Scenario: A classmate is explaining a problem but keeps repeating themselves. Write a response that shows you're listening and helps them move forward.

_____

_____

_____

Module 8
Leadership Activity Guide

Scoop of the day

What is leadership?

Leadership means guiding, inspiring, and motivating others to reach a common goal.

☑ Clear communication

☑ Smart decision-making

☑ Problem-solving

☑ Adaptability

Why does it matter?

How does leadership help in life or work?

- Build trust and respect.
- Keep teams on track.
- Succeed—especially in workplaces that use AI and new technology.

Think...

How can leadership skills give you an edge at work?

_____

_____

Mind expeditions

Role-play Activity: Act out a short scene where a group is in utter chaos and struggling with no direction. Then "rewind" and show how someone stepping up can guide and motive the group into the right direction. Reflect on what changed and how it was more effective:

What would you do?

Scenario: You lead a team on an urgent project. Two teammates, Emma and John, are clashing and slowing progress.

1. Ignore the conflict and hope it resolves.

2. Meet with them separately, then help them find common ground.

3. Tell the team to focus and not let personal issues interfere.

Your choice? Why...?

_____

_____

Real-world examples...

Healthcare: A head nurse delegates tasks during a busy shift.

Construction: A foreman keeps projects on schedule.

Corporate: A manager motivates teams during big changes.

Write an example!

Describe a time when leadership helped a team succeed.

_____

_____

AI Prompt Exercise...

Write an AI prompt that is clear, specific, and detailed enough to help you get the best possible answer.

Scenario: Describe a time-crunch situation and ask AI for solutions; choose the best one and explain why.

_____

_____

Module 9
Time Management Activity Guide

Scoop of the day

What is time management?

Time management means organizing tasks, using time wisely, and meeting deadlines.

- ☑ Planning ahead
- ☑ Staying organized
- ☑ Self-discipline

Why does it matter?

How does time management help in life or work?

- Get more done with less stress.
- Meet deadlines and goals.
- Standout—especially when working with AI and technology tools.

Think...

How does time management give you an advantage at work?

_____

_____

Mind expeditions

Simulation: _Beat the clock!_ Assign tasks, set deadlines, and track your progress. What did you learn?

What would you do?

Scenario: You have several deadlines:

- A report due today.
- A meeting in an hour.
- A presentation for tomorrow.

Your manager just gave you another urgent task. Now what?

- How do you prioritize?
- What helps you stay calm and focused?
- How do you talk to your manager if you need help or deadline changes?

💬 Write your ideas....

_____

_____

Real-world examples...

Education: Teachers balance grading and planning.

Corporate: Project managers juggle multiple deadlines.

Freelancing: Designers manage different clients at once.

Write an example!

Describe a time you used time management to meet a goal.

_____

_____

AI Prompt Exercise...

Write an AI prompt that is clear, specific, and detailed enough to help you get the best possible answer.

Scenario: You realize you're spending too much time on social media and not enough on homework. Ask AI for three strategies to stay focused and manage distractions.

_____

_____

Module 10
Adaptability Activity Guide

Scoop of the day

What is adaptability?

Adaptability means adjusting to changes, challenges, or surprises with a positive attitude and flexibility.

- ☑ Resilience

- ☑ Problem-solving

- ☑ Openness to learning

Why does it matter?

How does adaptability help in life or work?

- Stay productive under pressure.
- Handling unexpected problems.
- Succeed—especially in workplaces driven by AI and constant change.

Think...

How can adaptability give you an advantage in your career?

_____

_____

Mind expeditions

Roleplay: In a group, act out a short scene where plans suddenly change and cause problems. Then "rewind" and showcase how the adaptability techniques we learned can help solve the issues. Reflect on what changed and how it was more effective below:

What would you do?

Scenario: You're a nurse in a busy hospital, assigned to a department you don't know well. Patient needs are urgent, and help is limited. How do you prioritize?

- How do you adjust quickly while staying safe?

- How do you stay calm?

- How do you ask for help without disrupting others?

💭 Write your ideas....

_____

_____

Real-world examples...

Chef: Swaps ingredients when deliveries fail.

Software Developer: Pivots when project requirements change.

Teacher: Changes lesson plans when technology goes down.

Write an example!

Describe a time you adapted to a challenge.

_____

_____

AI Prompt Exercise...

Write an AI prompt that is clear, specific, and detailed enough to help you get the best possible answer.

Scenario: Your summer job changes your schedule at the last minute. Outline how you'd manage school, work, and activities.

_____

_____

Module 11
Networking Activity Guide

Scoop of the day

What is networking?

Networking means creating and maintaining connections that help you grow personally and professionally.

- [x] Communication

- [x] Building trust

- [x] Offering and receiving support

Why does it matter?

How does adaptability help in life or work?

- Learn about new opportunities.
- Gain support and advice.
- Grow your career faster, especially with AI tools that help you connect online.

Think...

How can networking help you reach your goals?

_____

_____

Mind expeditions

Role-Play Activity: You're at a school event with professionals you don't know. How will you start a conversation and make a positive impression?

What would you do?

Scenario: You're at a corporate conference full of industry leaders and potential partners. You feel nervous about introducing yourself.

- How do you confidently approach new people?

- How do you make real connections, not just swap cards?

- How do you follow up after the event?

Write your ideas....

_____

_____

Real-world examples...

Entrepreneur: Meets an investor, shares their vision, and schedules a funding meeting.

Marketing Specialist: Builds relationships with influencers for partnerships.

IT Professional: Engages in online forums and gets job offers.

Write an example!

Describe a time when networking helped you or someone you know.

_____

_____

AI Prompt Exercise...

Write an AI prompt that is clear, specific, and detailed enough to help you get the best possible answer.

Scenario: Ask AI to create a short message you could send to a local professional you admire, introducing yourself and expressing interest in learning from them.

_____

_____

Module 12
Creativity Activity Guide

Scoop of the day

What is creativity?

Creativity is generating new ideas, thinking outside the box, and finding innovative solutions.

☑ Imagination

☑ Problem-solving

☑ Seeing connections others might miss

Why does it matter?

How does creativity help in life or work?

- Solving problems in unique ways.
- Stand out in any career.
- Innovate—especially when using AI and new technology.

Think...

How can creativity help you succeed in your career?

_____

_____

Mind expeditions

Mind Map: Pick a problem in your community. In the space below, create a mind map of a product or service that could help solve it.

🧠 What would you do?

Scenario: You've started a small business, but sales are low. Traditional marketing isn't working, and your budget is tight.

- How can you think creatively to reach more customers?

- What low-cost or unique strategies could you try?

- How can you test ideas without big risks?

💬 Write your ideas....

_____

_____

Real-world examples...

Graphic Designer: Creates a viral social media campaign.

Engineer: Finds an innovative way to cut costs.

Teacher: Designs gamified lessons to boost engagement.

Write an example!

Describe a time when creativity made a difference.

_____

_____

AI Prompt Exercise...

Write an AI prompt that is clear, specific, and detailed enough to help you get the best possible answer.

Scenario: Ask AI to give you five unique ideas for a school fundraiser that no one has tried before, then pick one and explain how you would make it happen.

_____

_____

_____

Module 13
Empathy Activity Guide

Scoop of the day

What is empathy?

Empathy means understanding and sharing the feelings of others.

- ☑ Listening carefully

- ☑ Showing compassion

- ☑ Responding with care and respect

Why does it matter?

How does empathy help in life or work?

- Build trust and respect.
- Improve teamwork and leadership.
- Support others—especially in stressful times.

🧠 Think...

How can empathy help you succeed in your career?

_____

_____

Mind expeditions

Role-play Activity: In a group, act out a short scene where someone feels left out or misunderstood, causing tension. Then "rewind" and show how understanding their feelings can positively change the outcome. Reflect on what changed and how it was more effective:

What would you do?

Scenario: You're a manager. Your team member, Alex, is missing deadlines and seems distracted. In a private meeting, Alex shares that they're dealing with a family crisis.

1. Reprimand Alex for not handling personal issues better.

2. Listen with empathy, adjust deadlines, and offer support.

3. Ignore it and expect performance to improve.

Your choice? Why...?

_____

_____

Real-world examples...

Doctor: Listens to patients and provides support.

Customer Service: Helps upset customers calmly.

Manager: Adjusts workloads to support employees.

Write an example!

Describe a time when empathy helped a situation.

_____

_____

AI Prompt Exercise...

Write an AI prompt that is clear, specific, and detailed enough to help you get the best possible answer.

Scenario: Describe a school situation from one student's point of view, then ask AI to rewrite it from the perspective of another student involved.

_____

_____

Module 14
Digital Footprint Activity Guide

Scoop of the day

What is a digital footprint?

A digital footprint is the record of everything a person shares or does online.

☑ Responsibility

☑ Thoughtful choices

☑ Maintaining a positive online reputation

Why does it matter?

How does a digital footprint help in life or work?

- Shapes your reputation.
- Affects hiring, college admissions, and networking.
- Build credibility.

Think...

How can maintaining a good digital footprint help you succeed in your career?

_____

_____

Mind expeditions

Think-Pair-Share: Share imaginative solutions with a partner, refine together, then present to the class about maintaining a professional digital footprint. Write below what you learned.

What would you do?

Scenario: You've launched a small business, but sales are low and your budget is tight. Traditional marketing isn't working, so you need a creative, low-cost way to attract customers and grow.

- How can you think outside the box to market your business effectively?

- What low-cost or unconventional strategies could help you reach your target audience?

- How do you test new ideas while managing risks?

Write your ideas...

_____

_____

Real-world examples...

Graphic Designer: A designer creates a viral social media campaign that brings massive engagement to a brand.

Engineer: An engineer finds an innovative way to reduce production costs while maintaining quality.

Write an example!

Describe a time when digital footprint has influenced a situation:

_____

_____

AI Prompt Exercise...

Write an AI prompt that is clear, specific, and detailed enough to help you get the best possible answer.

Scenario: Imagine a future employer looks at your social media profile. Write three posts or updates you'd want them to see that highlight your strengths.

_____

_____

The mystical world of artificial intelligence

Can AI replace people's skills?

Artificial Intelligence (AI) has changed the way we live and work. It's great at handling tasks that rely on technical skills- like organizing data or automating processes- which can make work faster and easier. But with AI taking over many of these tasks, how can you make sure your job is secure in the future?

Here's the truth

AI can't replace human connections.

AI can't fully understand emotions, build relationships, or lead a team with empathy. Think about it- why do people get frustrated when they can't talk to a real person on the phone? Or when ChatGPT doesn't quite "get" what you're asking? That's because humans want to be heard, understood, and supported- something only people can offer.

AI is a powerful tool, but your **soft skills**- like communication, teamwork, leadership, and empathy- are what make you stand out. To succeed, you need to know how to use AI and strengthen your people skills. The best leaders of the future will know how to do both.

Your input → Determines your output

World of AI Activities

How would you....

Ask ChatGPT about starting your own business as a teenager? List different ways to ask!

_____

_____

_____

Ask ChatGPT about choosing the right college for you? List different ways to ask!

_____

_____

_____

Ask ChatGPT about alternatives to college? List different ways to ask!

_____

_____

_____

Ask ChatGPT to draft an email to an employee about being late? List different ways to ask!

_____

_____

_____

Ask ChatGPT to draft an email to an employee about not doing a task correctly? List different ways to ask!

_____

_____

_____

Notes

_____

_____

_____

_____

_____

_____

_____

_____

_____

_____

_____

_____

_____

_____

Notes